Discover Planets

Discover

Venus

Margaret J. Goldstein

Lerner Publications ◆ Minneapolis

Lerner Publications Company
A division of Lerner Publishing Group, Inc.
241 First Avenue North
Minneapolis, MN 55401 USA

For reading levels and more information, look up this title at www.lernerbooks.com.

Main body text set in Adrianna Regular 14/20.
Typeface provided by Chank.

Library of Congress Cataloging-in-Publication Data

Names: Goldstein, Margaret J., author.
Title: Discover Venus / Margaret J. Goldstein.
Description: Minneapolis : Lerner Publications, [2018] | Series: Searchlight books.
    Discover planets | Audience: Ages 8–11. | Audience: Grades 4 to 6. | Includes
    bibliographical references and index.
Identifiers: LCCN 2017061817 (print) | LCCN 2017053543 (ebook) |
    ISBN 9781541525481 (eb pdf) | ISBN 978 9781541523401 (lb : alk. paper) |
    ISBN 9781541527911 (pb : alk. paper)
Subjects: LCSH: Venus (Planet)—Exploration—Juvenile literature. | Venus (Planet)—
    Juvenile literature.
Classification: LCC QB621 (print) | LCC QB621 .G6595 2018 (ebook) | DDC 523.42—dc23

LC record available at https://lccn.loc.gov/2017061817

Manufactured in the United States of America
1-44413-34672-2/22/2018

Contents

Chapter 1

WELCOME TO VENUS

From Earth, the planet Venus looks pretty. It shines softly in the evening sky. It has a whitish-yellow glow. It's named for the Roman goddess of love.

But if you could visit Venus, you wouldn't love it there. The temperature on its surface is almost 900°F (482°C). Venus is the hottest planet in the solar system. The clouds there are made of acid.

Other than the moon and the sun, Venus (*top center*) is the brightest object in the sky.

If you could spend a day on Venus, you'd be there a long time. A day is the time it takes for a planet to rotate once. A day on Earth takes twenty-four hours. But a day on Venus takes 243 Earth days. That's the slowest rotation of any planet in the solar system. Scientists think the pull of the sun's gravity may be part of the reason why Venus rotates so slowly.

A year is the time it takes for a planet to orbit the sun once. One year on Venus takes 224.7 Earth days. A day on Venus is longer than one year there because of how slowly the planet rotates.

Venus rotates in the opposite direction of Earth and most other planets.

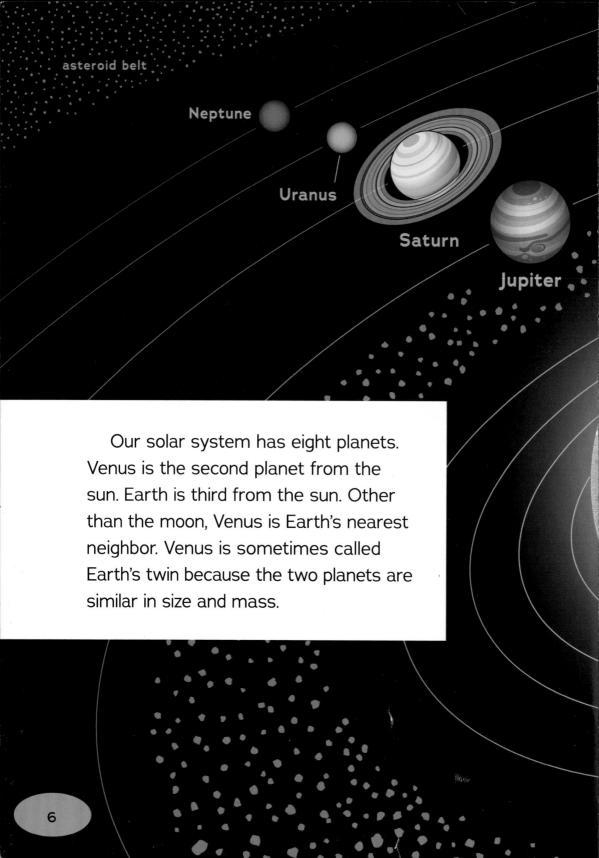

asteroid belt

Neptune

Uranus

Saturn

Jupiter

Our solar system has eight planets. Venus is the second planet from the sun. Earth is third from the sun. Other than the moon, Venus is Earth's nearest neighbor. Venus is sometimes called Earth's twin because the two planets are similar in size and mass.

The Solar System

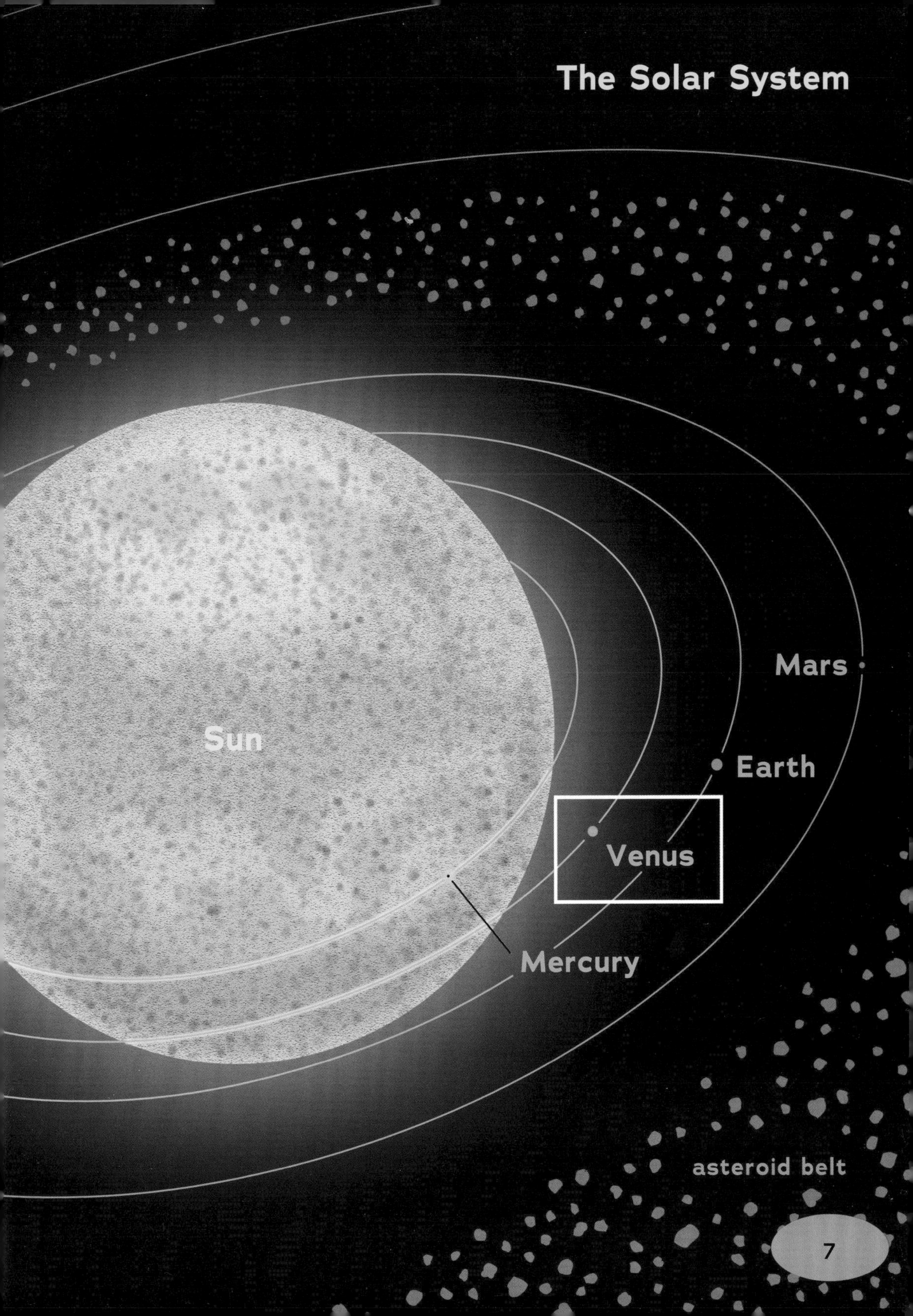

Sun

Mars

Earth

Venus

Mercury

asteroid belt

Venus doesn't give off light on its own. It reflects light from the sun. When viewed through a telescope, Venus sometimes looks like a circle of light. Other times, it looks like a half circle or a crescent.

For about nine months, Venus shines in Earth's eastern sky before sunrise. Then for another nine months, Venus shines in the western sky after sunset. But sometimes, we can't see Venus at all.

Why does Venus seem to change shape and appear at different times and places? Venus and Earth orbit the sun on different paths and at different speeds. Venus's appearance on a certain day depends on the position of Venus, Earth, and the sun on that day.

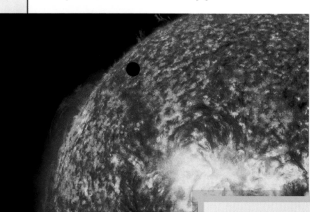

Venus looks like a black dot when it passes in front of the sun.

Chapter 2

HOT SPOT

Venus is burning hot. Deep inside Venus is a core of red-hot iron. Outside the core is a thick layer of melted rock. Venus's outer layer, or crust, is also made of rock. The rocks on Venus's surface are blazing hot, like embers in a fireplace.

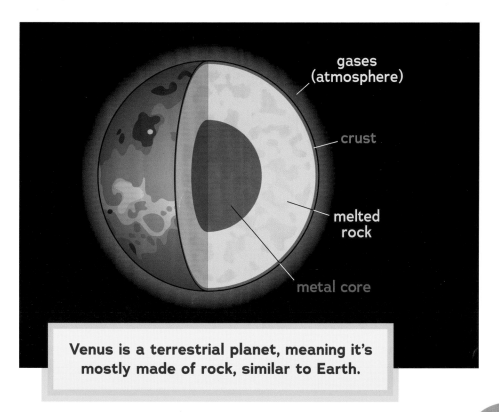

gases (atmosphere)

crust

melted rock

metal core

Venus is a terrestrial planet, meaning it's mostly made of rock, similar to Earth.

Weather Forecast

Venus's atmosphere has two main layers. Near the ground, the air is filled mostly with carbon dioxide. This is a clear gas. Above that is a layer of clouds about 12 miles (20 km) thick. The clouds are not made of water like clouds on Earth. They're made of sulfuric acid.

The thick atmosphere makes it difficult to see Venus's surface. Scientists use radar to help them view beneath the clouds. Radar systems use reflected radio waves to build a picture of an object.

Sulfuric acid clouds give Venus its yellow color.

ON THE GROUND, VENUS MIGHT LOOK SIMILAR TO EARTH ON AN OVERCAST DAY.

It rains on Venus, but the raindrops aren't made of water. They're made of sulfuric acid, just like the clouds. Because the planet is so hot, the raindrops evaporate before they reach the ground.

The winds are gentle near the ground on Venus. But high in the atmosphere, the winds are ferocious. They can blow faster than 200 miles (322 km) per hour. Fierce winds blow like hurricanes around Venus's north and south poles.

Venus's atmosphere is extremely heavy. The air pressure on Venus is ninety times greater than the pressure on Earth.

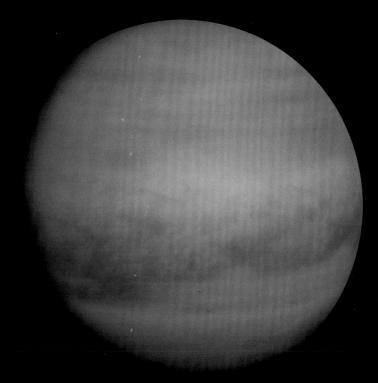

Air pressure is the weight of the atmosphere pressing down on the ground.

Ground Level

Venus has tall mountains and deep canyons. The highest mountain range, Maxwell Montes, is taller than Mount Everest, Earth's highest mountain. Venus also has bowl-shaped craters. They formed when asteroids and comets hit the planet.

SCIENTISTS ADDED COLOR TO RADAR IMAGES TO CREATE THIS PHOTO OF MAXWELL MONTES.

Many places on Venus have strange formations. These are places where lava from deep underground has oozed to the surface through volcanoes. The lava has hardened into different shapes. They look like rings, tiles, pancakes, and even spiders. Some volcanic formations are hundreds of millions of years old.

Venus has the most volcanoes of all the planets in our solar system. Scientists used information collected with radar to create this photo.

STEM Highlight

Venus's atmosphere is like the glass roof of a greenhouse. In a greenhouse, the roof traps energy from the sun, so the plants inside stay warm.

On Venus, sunlight travels through the atmosphere and warms the planet. Carbon dioxide is a heat-trapping gas. Because of all the carbon dioxide on Venus, the sun's heat cannot escape back into space. So Venus is extremely hot.

Earth's atmosphere acts like a greenhouse too. But Earth's air has much less carbon dioxide than Venus's air. This makes the temperatures on Earth much cooler than on Venus.

Even though Mercury is the closest planet to the sun, Venus (*right*) is hotter because of its atmosphere.

Chapter 3

ZOOMING IN ON VENUS

People have always wanted to know more about the universe. Thousands of years ago in Babylon, astronomers watched Venus. They noted when it appeared in the

morning sky and when it appeared in the evening sky. They tracked the dates for twenty-one years and wrote them on a clay tablet.

People in ancient Greece also watched Venus. They thought it was two different objects: a morning star and an evening star.

Ancient Babylonians wrote about Venus on the Venus tablet of Ammisaduqa.

A Planet for the Gods

In ancient times, people thought Venus was beautiful and magical. The Babylonians named it for their goddess of love: Ishtar. The ancient Romans named it for their own love goddess: Venus. In China, the planet was called Tai-pe, which means "beautiful white one."

The Mayans lived in ancient Mexico. They built an observatory for watching the sun and Venus. Mayan priests recorded Venus's movements in a book. To the Mayans, Venus was the god of war.

The Mayans watched Venus and other objects in the sky at this observatory.

Looking Closer

In 1610, Galileo Galilei looked at Venus through a telescope. This new invention gave him a close-up view of Venus. He saw its thick, yellow clouds. He made drawings of its changing phases. After Galileo, other astronomers studied Venus with telescopes. They watched its orbit and rotation.

Some early astronomers thought that everything in the solar system revolved around Earth. Galileo's studies of Venus helped prove that the sun, not Earth, is at the center of our solar system.

Galileo Galilei was an Italian astronomer.

Venus's clouds make it reflect more sunlight than other planets in the solar system.

In the early twentieth century, astronomers studied light coming from Venus. By analyzing the light, researchers determined that Venus has carbon dioxide in its atmosphere. In the 1960s, astronomers used radar to look beneath Venus's thick layer of clouds. They discovered mountains and valleys on the planet's surface.

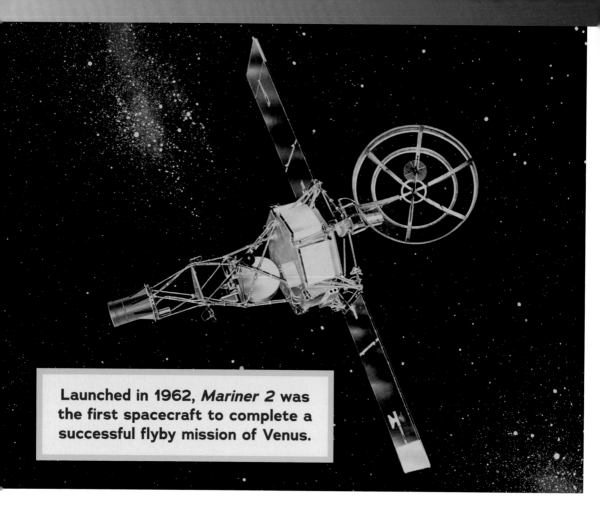

Launched in 1962, *Mariner 2* was the first spacecraft to complete a successful flyby mission of Venus.

The Space Age

In the 1960s, the US National Aeronautics and Space Administration (NASA) began sending spacecraft to Venus. The Soviet Union, a former group of republics including Russia, did as well. The spacecraft carried cameras and scientific instruments. They took photographs and measured light, gases, and radiation on Venus. The spacecraft sent these pictures and measurements back to scientists on Earth.

Some spacecraft orbited the planet. Others just flew past it. Several spacecraft landed on Venus. They took photographs, made temperature readings, and studied Venus's soil. But the spacecraft didn't operate for long. Venus's fierce heat melted them. The atmosphere's heavy pressure crushed them. The longest any craft lasted on Venus was 127 minutes.

Venera 1 **flew by Venus in the 1960s, but the spacecraft broke down before it was able to send back any data.**

STEM Highlight

The plants and animals that live on Earth could not survive on Venus. They'd burn up in the heat. But high in the clouds above Venus, the temperatures are about the same as temperatures on Earth. The sulfuric acid in the clouds is deadly to people but not to some tiny organisms on Earth. Scientists think that similar creatures could survive in Venus's clouds. This is just a theory. Scientists haven't found any evidence of life on Venus.

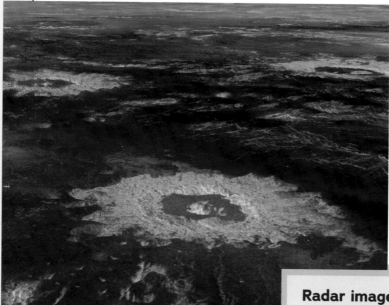

Radar images of Venus have failed to turn up evidence of life.

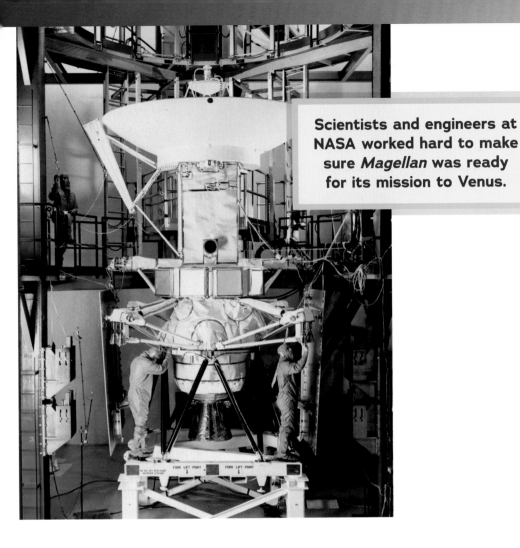

Scientists and engineers at NASA worked hard to make sure *Magellan* was ready for its mission to Venus.

From 1990 to 1994, NASA's *Magellan* spacecraft orbited Venus. Using radar, *Magellan* mapped 98 percent of Venus's surface. It showed mountains, valleys, craters, volcanoes, and other land features.

The International Astronomical Union (IAU) gave names to some of the planet's features. Since Venus is named for a goddess, almost all the names came from goddesses and female heroes of many cultures.

Chapter 4

EXPRESS TO VENUS

In 2005, the European Space Agency launched a spacecraft called *Venus Express.* The craft reached Venus in 2006. It orbited the planet until it ran out of fuel in 2014. It then fell into Venus's atmosphere and burned up. It carried state-of-the-art instruments. *Venus Express* made some fascinating discoveries.

Venus Express's instruments analyzed Venus's temperature, radiation, atmosphere, surface, and volcanoes.

Using observations of clouds made by *Venus Express*, researchers tracked the planet's wind speeds.

Wild and Windy

Venus Express measured the winds in Venus's upper atmosphere. The winds were speeding up. When the spacecraft arrived in 2006, the winds reached a top speed of 186 miles (300 km) per hour. By the end of the mission, the top speed was 248 miles (400 km) per hour. Scientists don't know why the wind speeds increased.

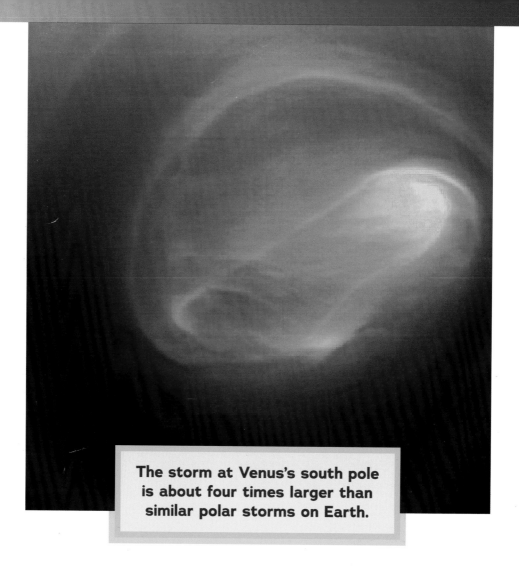

The storm at Venus's south pole is about four times larger than similar polar storms on Earth.

The spacecraft also took a close look at a powerful storm at Venus's south pole. Sometimes the storm swirls in a circle or oval. It also moves in other directions. It zigzags and spins up and down. Sometimes its path looks like the letter *S*, a figure eight, or another shape. It changes all the time. Astronomers haven't seen a storm like this on any other planet.

The Next Visit

The United States and Russia hope to work together on a mission called Venera-D. The mission will include several vehicles. One will land on Venus. Another will orbit the planet. The mission might include a spacecraft that flies through Venus's atmosphere.

What new secrets will the mission uncover? Will it find evidence of life on Venus?

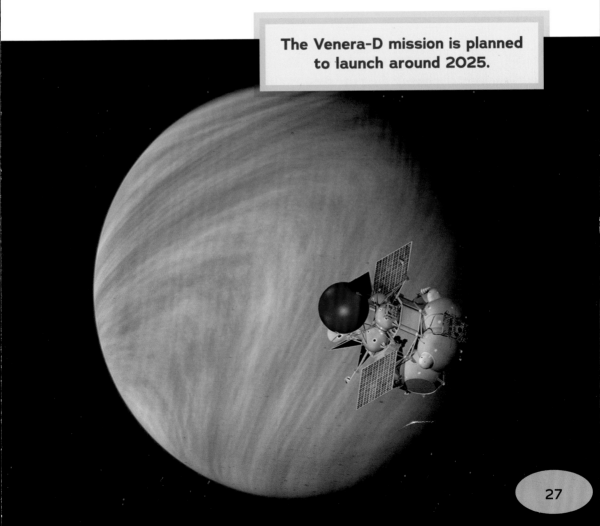

The **Venera-D mission is planned to launch around 2025.**

STEM Highlight

Scientists think that about three billion years ago, Venus had oceans full of water. It was also much cooler. Its temperatures were lower than those on Earth. It might have been possible for life to form there.

Over millions of years, the sun's heat caused the planet's water to evaporate. This evaporation led to chemical changes in the atmosphere. More carbon dioxide built up in the air. The carbon dioxide trapped even more heat from the sun. The planet became hotter and hotter.

This illustration shows what the surface on Venus may look like.

Looking Ahead

- *Venus Express* found flashes of lightning in Venus's clouds. On Earth, the movement of water inside clouds creates lightning. Scientists believe that the sulfuric acid in Venus's clouds may cause its lightning. Astronomers hope to learn more about how this lightning forms.

- Engineers want to build a vehicle that can explore Venus's surface for a long time. It will need to be superstrong to withstand the planet's high temperature and crushing air pressure. Engineers are testing models by baking them in ovens.

- Some scientists envision a human colony on Venus. They say people could live safely inside giant balloons floating through Venus's clouds. If this were possible, would you sign up to live there?

Glossary

astronomer: a person who studies objects and forces outside Earth's atmosphere, such as planets, stars, and energy traveling through space

atmosphere: a layer of gases surrounding a planet, a moon, or another object in space

evaporate: to turn from a liquid into a gas

gravity: the force that pulls things toward the center of an object in space (such as a planet, moon, or sun) and keeps them from floating away

mass: the amount of material in an object

observatory: a building or place designed for watching objects in the sky

orbit: to travel around another object in an oval or circular path

phase: one of the different appearances of a planet or moon that people see on Earth as the object travels through space

radar: a system that sends out radio waves for detecting and mapping an object by the reflection of the radio waves

radiation: energy that takes the form of waves or particles

rotate: to spin around a centerline, like a spinning top

solar system: a group consisting of a star and the planets and other objects that orbit the star. In our solar system, the star is called the sun.

Learn More about Venus

Books

Kruesi, Liz. *Discover Space Exploration*. Minneapolis: Lerner Publications, 2017. How do astronomers study planets like Venus? They send remote-controlled spacecraft and rovers to do the exploring. Learn all about these projects here.

Payment, Simone. *Venus*. New York: Britannica Educational, 2017. Venus is called Earth's twin, but the two planets are very different. This book explores the latest discoveries about Venus.

Wilkins, Mary-Jane. *The Inner Planets*. Tucson, AZ: Brown Bear Books, 2017. Mercury, Venus, Earth, and Mars are the inner planets of the solar system. Learn all about Venus and its closest neighbors.

Websites

Mission to Venus
https://kids.nationalgeographic.com/explore/space/mission-to-venus/
Visit this website to learn more about Venus and to find links to information about the rest of the solar system and outer space.

NASA Space Place
https://spaceplace.nasa.gov/menu/play/
This website from NASA includes games, activities, and articles that let you explore Earth and space.

Solar System 101
https://solarsystem.nasa.gov/kids/index.cfm
This NASA website lets you explore the sun, planets, moons, and other objects in our solar system.

Index

Photo Acknowledgments

The images in this book are used with the permission of: ESO/B. Tafreshi (twanight.org), p. 4; NASA/JPL, pp. 5, 14, 15, 20, 22; Laura Westlund/Independent Picture Service, pp. 6–7, 9; NASA/SDO, AIA (CC BY 2.0), p. 8; NASA, pp. 10, 23; David P. Anderson, Southern Methodist University/NASA/Science Source, pp. 11, 13; manjik/Shutterstock.com, p. 12; Fæ/Wikimedia Commons (CC BY-SA 3.0), p. 16; Arian Zwegers/Wikimedia Commons (CC BY 2.0), p. 17; Hulton Archive/Getty Images, p. 18; Detlev van Ravenswaay/Science Source, p. 19; Sovfoto/Universal Images Group/Getty Images, p. 21; ESA-J.L Atteleyn, p. 24; ESA-D. DUCROS, p. 25; ESA/VIRTIS/INAF-IASF/Obs. de Paris-LESIA/Univ. Oxford, p. 26; NASA/JPL-Caltech, p. 27; Julian Baum/Science Source, p. 28.

Cover: NASA/JPL.